It's **NATURE!**

S E R I E S

Ferocious Fangs

12 OF NATURE'S MOST AMAZING ANIMALS

by Sally Fleming

NORTHWORD PRESS

Minnetonka, Minnesota

DEDICATION

For Danny Aupi, a champion hunter of fossil shark's teeth

© NorthWord Press, 2001

Photography © 2001 by: Norbert Wu/www.norbertwu.com: cover, pp. 3, 19, 27; E. R. Degginger/Dembinsky Photo Assoc.: p. 4; Brian Kenney: pp. 7, 9, 17, 21, 31; Brian Parker/Tom Stack & Associates: p. 11; Mike Bacon/Tom Stack & Associates: p. 13; Gary Milburn/Tom Stack & Associates: p. 15; James D. Watt/Innerspace Visions: p. 23; Gary Mezaros/Dembinsky Photo Assoc.: p. 25; John Shaw/Tom Stack & Associates: p. 29

NorthWord Press
5900 Green Oak Dr
Minnetonka, MN 55343
1-800-328-3895

Book design by Russell S. Kuepper
Illustrated by Kay Underwood
Edited by Barbara K. Harold

Library of Congress Cataloging-in-Publication Data
Ferocious fangs / Sally Fleming ; illustrations by Kay Underwood.
    p. cm. — (It's nature! series)
ISBN 1-55971-587-1 (softcover)
1. Fangs—Juvenile literature. [1. Fangs.] I. Underwood, Kay, ill.
II. Title. III. Series.
QL858.F54 2001
591.47-dc21   00-045572

Printed in Malaysia
10 9 8 7 6 5 4 3 2 1

CONTENTS

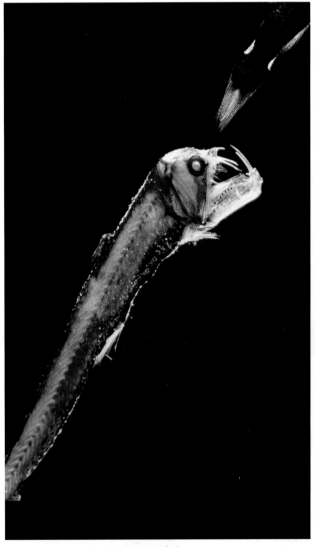

Viperfish

ABOUT FANGS

Have you ever worn fun false teeth with sharp points as part of a costume? If you have, your false teeth may have scared some people. Maybe you pretended to be a hungry shark. But instead of using the teeth to frighten people, you just used them to bite off a piece of sandwich!

Bush Viper

Many animals have sharply pointed teeth. They use them while fighting **predators** (animals that would eat them). Sharp teeth are great for stabbing into a likely meal and holding it tightly. Some teeth are much larger and their points are sharper than others. Scientists call these kinds of teeth fangs.

All fangs are used for biting and gripping **prey** (animals eaten as food). But animals have different types of fangs. Some fish and mammals use their fangs for ripping apart food. These fangs sink deeply into prey. They let the animal tear off chunks of meat into smaller bites that can be swallowed.

Some animals have deadly fangs. Their pointy tips inject **venom** (poison) into prey. Certain venoms act on the prey's nervous system. They stop the messages sent by a prey's nerves to important muscles. When muscles around lungs are stopped, for example, an animal can no longer breathe. Different venoms act on the prey's heart and blood. They make the prey's heart stop beating, by causing the walls of tiny blood vessels to break apart. Whichever way a venom works, the prey usually dies.

Scientists believe that the animal fangs we see today are the result of small changes that took place over thousands or millions of years. These fangs have helped animals develop effective ways to catch or kill prey, or are useful for frightening away predators.

The creatures in this book use their fangs almost every day. Their fangs may be very short, like those belonging to a tiny shrew. Or they may be large, like the jagged-edged teeth of a great white shark. You'll meet spiders and snakes with venomous fangs and a fish with fangs so large they overlap its jaws. Some of the fangs you'll learn about are scary. Some of them look weird. But no matter how strange or scary we may think these fangs are, they are very important to the animal. It needs them to survive.

RATTLING REPTILES

The eastern diamondback (Crotalus adamanteus) is found only in the United States. It lives mainly in the southeast, from North Carolina to Florida, and as far west as Mississippi. The eastern diamondback lives in pine woods and places with palmetto shrubs. It finds shelter in rocky areas and places where dried leaves litter the ground. It may live near swamps, but stays in places where the ground is high and dry.

When people almost bump into you, you probably warn them by saying, "Watch out!" A rattlesnake warns with its tail. The warning buzz from an eastern diamondback rattlesnake has made many people move farther away—fast!

Eastern diamondback rattlesnakes are the largest of the 32 **species** (kinds) of rattlers. They average 4 to 5 feet (122 to 152 cm) long, but can grow up to 6 feet (183 cm).

Their name comes from the beautiful pattern formed by the snake's overlapping scales. A thin band of cream-colored scales outlines dark brown diamonds on the snake's back.

The snake's rattle is made of **keratin** (the same material that makes your fingernails). A rattler sheds its skin 2 or 3 times per year. All the old skin comes off except for the segment, or piece, containing the scale on the tail's tip. This is the piece that remains as the rattle.

Each time the snake sheds, a new segment is added to the rattle. The new segment partly covers the old segment above it. That keeps the loose, older segment from falling off.

When the rattler shakes its tail, the old segments rattle against each other and make the buzzing noise.

In warm weather, an eastern diamondback rattler's tail shakes very quickly. Its buzzing sound can be heard many yards (meters) away. Whenever temperatures are cool, the rattle shakes more slowly. When a rattle gets too long, the oldest segments break off.

Most of the time, a rattler relies on its coloring to hide from a predator. If possible, it crawls away. When it really feels threatened, the snake rattles. Scientists think the rattle evolved to warn large animals, like bison, to move away. If ignored, a fang bite is likely to follow! But biting to defend itself is a rattler's last resort.

A rattler's fangs may grow up to 1 inch (2.5 cm) long. When a rattler strikes, its fangs swing down and out, like a hinge. The snake's head darts forward. Its fangs stab into the victim. A rattler's fangs are hollow, like hypodermic needles. When they sink into prey, the snake squeezes the muscles surrounding the venom glands located inside its head. Amber-colored venom flows through a tube into the fang's hollow opening and squirts out the tip.

After biting, the rattler folds its fangs back toward the roof of its mouth. A fleshy covering on the fangs keeps them from pricking the snake.

The snake swallows its prey whole. A rattler has smaller, sharp teeth in the bones behind its fangs and in its bottom jaw. They keep the prey's body from slipping while the snake swallows.

People can survive the bite of an eastern diamondback rattlesnake. But the venom is very strong, so anyone who is bitten must go to a hospital quickly. Doctors can treat them with **antivenin** (a special medicine made to combat a snake's venom). But the best thing to do if you see a snake, is to leave it alone. The eastern diamondback rattlesnake would really much rather use its fangs on prey, such as a rabbit, mouse, or lizard.

FANTASTIC FACT!

Eastern diamondbacks are land-dwelling snakes. However, they can swim well in either fresh or salt water. In fact, eastern diamondbacks have been spotted in the ocean, several miles (kilometers) away from land!

BLACK WIDOW SPIDERS

Black widow spiders (Latrodectus mactans) can be found worldwide. Five species live in the United States. They are found in every state except for Alaska and Hawaii. Black widows often live on the underside of ledges or around rocks and woodpiles, or just about any place that a web can be strung. Cold weather and drought may drive these spiders into buildings, such as sheds, garages, and houses.

SHY SPINNERS

Imagine that your body is just a bit larger than your thumbnail. Now, pretend that you have two sharp fangs. What would you do if a giant brushed against your body? Most likely, you'd bite! That's exactly what a female black widow spider does.

Female black widows are dangerous. Their bite is very painful and can make a person extremely sick. Sometimes a bite causes death. A black widow's venom is 15 times more **potent** (strong) than some rattlesnake venom. Fortunately, females only inject a tiny amount of venom. Males do not bite at all and are harmless.

Many people wrongly think that black widows are vicious spiders. Black widows are really shy. They prefer to live in dark, sheltered places. Even when people go in or near these places, black widows don't jump out and try to bite them. Whenever possible, they crawl away or hide. They may even try playing dead. Bites usually occur because a person has brushed against the spider.

Adult female black widows are shiny and black. **Spiderlings** (babies) are white or yellowish, and darken as they grow. A red mark, shaped like an hourglass, develops on a female's **abdomen** (belly).

The red hourglass shape is a good way to identify a female black widow. Males are brown and may have stripes on their bodies. They are half the size, or less, of females.

A black widow sheds its hard outer skeleton as many as ten times in its life. If the spider is missing a leg, it regrows when the spider sheds.

Black widows do not hunt for food. A female hardly ever leaves her web. Instead, a female waits for prey to land in her web. The web is a tangle of sticky silk strands. The silky strands are produced by a spider's **spinnerets** (special glands on the end of a spider's abdomen). Any prey unlucky enough to land on the web gets stuck.

Black widows have eight eyes. But they don't see clearly. They can only distinguish light objects from dark ones. However, a black widow doesn't rely on her eyes to know when prey has been caught. Instead, vibrations from the prey's struggling body alert her. She waits until the prey animal wears itself out. Then, she quickly wraps the prey with her silky threads.

After wrapping the prey, she jabs it with her two fangs. She squeezes the muscles around her venom glands inside her head. Venom flows out and into her fangs. An opening in the tip of each fang lets venom slowly enter into the prey. In a short time, the prey dies.

The female also injects a liquid that turns the organs inside the prey's body into mushy goop. The black widow then sucks it out for her meal. A female black widow usually eats insects, but she can also eat centipedes and scorpions. Male black widows do not eat. In fact, they die within a few weeks of growing up and mating.

FANTASTIC FACT!

Once the spiderlings have hatched, they'd better watch out. Their mother will eat them if she gets the chance!

PIRANHAS

FEARSOME FEEDERS

There are at least twenty species of piranha in the world. The red-bellied piranha (Serrasalmus nattereri) lives in warm water in eastern and central South America. It can be found in large rivers such as the Amazon, Orinoco, and Paraña, and the smaller rivers that feed into them. Red-bellied piranhas are also found in lakes.

Have you ever read about goldminers panning for gold? They often wrote about their excitement at seeing gold flecks flashing in their pans. When you see a red-bellied piranha swimming in the light, the first thing you think is, "That fish is covered with gold!" But when its face turns toward you, you only notice its sharp fangs.

Sharp, white, triangular teeth line a red-bellied piranha's jaws. When the jaw is opened and closed, the teeth slide past each other. Like a scissors, they slice into a prey's body. A piranha relies on its sharp fangs to catch its meals. To remain sharp, the fangs are replaced every so often. Fangs are replaced on alternating sides of the jaw. This allows a piranha to continue feeding. A piranha is never left without any teeth.

Piranhas have a bloodthirsty, human-eating reputation. The truth is, they don't usually attack people. Many people swim and bathe regularly in water where piranhas live. Attacks do sometimes occur and the bites can be very nasty. If the attack is severe, hospitalization may be necessary, but victims have survived.

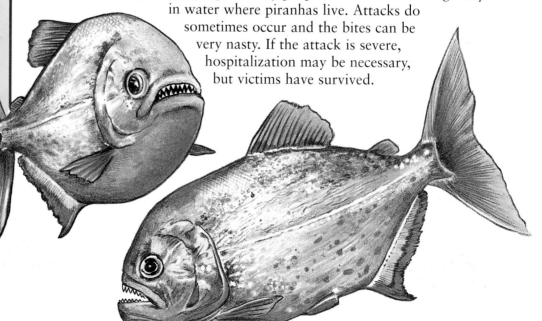

In fact, no one can accurately document a case where red-bellied piranhas have attacked and killed a healthy person. So why do they have such a bad reputation?

Scientists think it's because there are documented records of piranhas stripping the flesh from human skeletons. However, they believe these victims had drowned and were dead long before the piranhas attacked. And "water cleaner-upper" is a very important job for piranhas.

When rains are heavy, rivers and lakes often flood, killing many animals. Left untouched, the **carcasses** (dead bodies) rot in the water. That can make the water unhealthy for animal life. By cleaning the flesh from a carcass, piranhas help keep the water clean.

Red-bellied piranhas can grow up to 2 feet (61 cm) long. Sometimes they form **schools** (groups) of 30 to 40 fish. A school this size can quickly eat a cow's carcass. The water **roils** (bubbles up) when a hungry school feeds.

Piranhas hunt live prey, too. Young piranhas eat insects and small fishes. Adults eat larger fishes and smaller piranhas. Piranhas often nip scales and chunks of flesh or fins from their prey. After taking a single bite, they may leave the prey alone.

Cormorants and other water birds will eat piranhas, if they can catch them. People catch and eat piranhas, too.

FANTASTIC FACT!

A group of red-bellied piranhas can strip a chicken's carcass to its bones in less than 2 minutes.

GILA MONSTERS

Gila monsters (Heloderma suspectum) are very rare, and are only found in a few places, where they are protected. They live in southern Nevada; San Bernardino County, California (near the Nevada border); southwestern Utah; western and southern Arizona; southwestern New Mexico; and part of Mexico. The Mexican beaded lizard is the only other venomous lizard in the world.

CAREFUL CRAWLERS

When you think of monsters, you probably imagine towering creatures that relentlessly stalk their victims. Well, the gila monster is just the opposite. A gila monster spends most of its time resting or sleeping. When it is active, it moves very slowly. In fact, the gila monster is the slowest of all lizards.

It's easy to tell a gila monster from other lizards. The pattern and colors of its skin are very distinctive. The snout, chin, legs, and feet are black. Black marks and bands, on a yellow or orangish background cover the rest of the body.

The gila monster grows to a length of about 16 inches (40.6 cm). A fully grown gila monster may weigh up to 1½ pounds (680 g).

Gila monsters **hibernate** (stay in a sleep-like state) during the winter. They store fat in their tail during the summer and fall to nourish their body while hibernating.

After hibernation, gila monsters are hungry. A gila monster hunts in the daytime during the spring and fall.

In the summer, when daytime temperatures are too hot, it hunts in the evening or at night. A gila monster often walks long distances while looking for food.

A gila monster can't run in quick bursts of speed to catch prey, nor can it strike, like a snake. It **forages**, or crawls around looking for whatever food it can find. And once prey has been found, a gila monster's needle-sharp, venomous fangs grab and hold it.

A hunting gila monster senses prey with its snake-like tongue that flicks in and out constantly. Each flick is searching for chemical **scents** (odors) produced by prey. The tongue carries the scent into a gila monster's mouth.

Because it moves so slowly, a gila monster hunts prey that is unable to run away. It raids the nests of rabbits, rodents, and ground-dwelling birds and eats the eggs or young it finds.

Fangs in the bottom jaw have a thin groove. The edges of the groove are very sharp. They cut the wound larger, allowing more venom to enter.

A gila monster's venom glands are in its bottom jaw. Venom flows out between the lizard's lips and its teeth. When the venom reaches a fang, it flows into the groove. Prey is swallowed slowly, in gulps, and without a lot of chewing. Scientists think that gila monsters use their venom mostly as a defensive weapon.

When a predator, such as a coyote, threatens a gila monster, the lizard first tries to escape. If its **burrow** (underground tunnel home) is close, a gila monster crawls backward toward it. It tries to scare the predator by hissing and opening its mouth. It may lunge forward. If that doesn't scare the predator away, the gila monster bites.

A gila monster doesn't bite out chunks of flesh. Its teeth grip tightly and keep grinding and chewing. Chewing forces more venom into the wound. It is almost impossible to make a gila monster let go. They have been known to hang on for 15 minutes or longer. Fortunately, a gila monster bite is not usually deadly. It is painful and makes a person feel sick for several days. With a doctor's care, a healthy person will recover completely.

FANTASTIC FACT!

The scales on a gila monster look like beads. They are round, not flat like a snake's scales. The gila monster's closely packed scales form a tough outer covering. It's good protection from predators.

BLOODSUCKING BEASTS

There are three species of vampire bats. All of them live in the Western Hemisphere, but none live in the United States. The closest is the common vampire bat (Desmodus rotundus), which lives from northern Mexico to northern Argentina and central Chile. Vampires roost in caves, deserted buildings, old wells, and hollow trees. They don't seek out people, but their favorite prey often lives near them.

All those blood-sucking vampire stories about Dracula are just that—stories! And they are stories that have given vampire bats a bad name. For one thing, vampire bats don't turn into people. For another, they don't suck all the blood out of their victims. They only remove about 2 tablespoons (30 ml) of blood. And not by sucking it out.

Vampire bats are 3 to 3¾ inches (7.6 to 9.5 cm) long. They weigh about 1 ounce (28.4 g). During the day, vampire bats stay in their **roost**. The roost is a dimly lit, quiet place, where the bats won't be bothered.

A group of bats that lives together is called a **colony**. A colony of vampire bats is usually about 20 to 100 bats. Occasionally a colony may have as many as 2,000 members. Vampire bats sleep and rest in their roosts. Sleeping and grooming are done while hanging upside down. To groom itself, a vampire bat holds on with one foot. The other foot scrapes dirt from the bat's fur. Then the bat licks its foot clean.

Female vampire bats take care of their young for several months. For the first two weeks, the mother bat doesn't even leave her baby to hunt. Another female feeds her the same way a mother bird feeds her baby.

Vampire bats have very long thumbs. They use them for support and locomotion when they are walking or hopping on the ground.

A female that has eaten **regurgitates** (spits up) part of her meal into the mother bat's mouth.

Vampire bats hunt at night. They prey almost entirely on large mammals such as cattle, horses, and burros. Occasionally vampires use a sleeping person for a meal. They may bite toes, fingers, and even lips. The bite is almost painless and a sleeping victim seldom wakes up.

Vampires have no trouble spotting large prey in an open field. First, the bat chooses its victim. Next it lands on the victim, or nearby. Quietly, the vampire walks or hops closer to its victim. When it is ready, the bat flies up onto the animal. Then the bat searches for a good spot to bite. Sometimes the bat sees an old wound. If it bites there, the search only takes a few minutes. A search for a new spot to bite may take as long as 40 minutes.

The bat licks the spot it has chosen. If hair or feathers are in the way, the bat cuts them away with teeth on the side of its jaw. Finally, the vampire uses its two **incisors** (chisel-shaped cutting teeth in the front of the mouth) to nip out a piece of the prey's skin. After that, the bat's fang-like **canine** teeth bite into the prey, so the bat doesn't fall off while it is feeding.

Vampire saliva has chemicals in it that stop blood from clotting. When the saliva gets inside the wound, blood flows out easily. Sometimes a wound may trickle blood for several hours.

The vampire tongue has grooves along the sides and on the bottom. To get blood, a vampire bat sticks its tongue in and out of the wound. Blood runs into the grooves. Pulling the tongue out probably creates some suction. That helps bring even more blood into the bat's mouth. The bat feeds for up to 30 minutes. Sometimes the bat has eaten so much that it has trouble flying off!

A vampire's bite is not poisonous or fatal. However, vampires often carry rabies and other diseases that can kill or harm the victim.

BLACK MAMBAS

Black mambas (Dendroaspis polylepis) are one of the deadliest snakes on Earth. They live in open woodlands, savannas, and dry, brushy areas of many countries in southern Africa. They may be found in old termite mounds, tree stumps, empty animal burrows, and rocky outcrops. Mambas spend most of their time on the ground, but will sometimes climb trees in search of prey.

SWIFT SERPENTS

An unexpected encounter with any snake might leave you feeling a bit shaken, even if the snake is short and not venomous. Just imagine how you would feel if you encountered a black mamba.

They are slender snakes, up to 14 feet (4.3 m) long. They are listed in the *Guinness Book of Records* as the world's fastest snake. A black mamba can slither as fast as 7 to 12 miles (11 to 19 km) per hour. It also strikes fast. And its venom is extremely **toxic** (poisonous).

Black mambas don't seek people out. However, more people are building homes in the areas black mambas live. **Confrontations** (uncomfortable meetings) are almost unavoidable.

The black mamba is not really black. Its color ranges from dark gray to olive green. As soon as a black mamba opens its mouth, the reason for its name is obvious. The inside is black, or purplish-black. Its head has been described as "coffin shaped," and the eyes are large and round.

A black mamba often raises its head up off the ground to look around. Black mambas are shy snakes and get nervous quickly. If the snake feels threatened, it may flatten the muscles in its neck. Then it looks a bit like a cobra. It opens its mouth wide and hisses a long warning. Even a huge, thick-skinned elephant backs off when a black mamba behaves like this!

Black mambas are **diurnal** (daytime) hunters. They are especially fond of squirrels, but eat other small mammals and birds. A snake's striking distance is less than the length of its body. Because black mambas are so long, they can strike a victim up to 6 feet (1.8 m) away.

The fangs in a black mamba's mouth are fixed in place. They do not swing down from the roof of the mamba's mouth the way a rattlesnake's fangs do. All a black mamba has to do is open its mouth. Its fangs are ready to bite.

Compared to a rattler's fangs, a black mamba's fangs seem short. But they inject much more venom, often as much as 100 milligrams (0.0035 ounce). It only takes 10 to 15 milligrams of venom to kill a person. A mouse will die in about 5 seconds. A person will begin to feel the effect of a bite in less than half an hour. If untreated, death can occur in 4 to 7 hours. So any black mamba bite should be taken very seriously and treated by a doctor immediately.

Scientists are experimenting with black mamba venom. It can be modified and used as a painkiller, and may be useful in fighting diseases.

FANTASTIC FACT!

A black mamba can raise the front part of its body up off the ground—high enough to raise its head 3 to 4 feet (0.9 to 1.2 m) above the ground.

FANGTOOTHS

Fangtooths (Anoplogaster cornuta) are mid-water to deep-water fish. They are found in most oceans worldwide. The fangtooth's menacing and gruesome appearance has earned it the nickname "ogrefish."

Some of the earth's most unusual looking fishes live deep in the ocean. The fangtooth has one of the most ferocious appearances. Its upper and lower jaws both have large fangs. But it's easy to avoid running into a fangtooth. The only way you are likely to encounter one is by riding inside a special submarine called a **submersible**. Deep in the ocean, water squeezes around objects more tightly than it does near the surface. Without the protection of a submarine, the weight of the water would crush your body.

If you looked out the window of your submersible, you would notice something interesting. The deeper the submersible dives, the darker the surrounding water becomes. The sun's light only reaches down to about 650 feet (195 m). Deep water stops certain light rays. The water begins to look dark blue. By 3,300 feet (1,000 m), the water is very dark. Without the sun's heat, the water also gets colder. Cold, dark waters are the fangtooth's normal home. Adult fangtooths live where the water is 2,000 to 16,000 feet (610 to 4,877 m) deep. The water temperature at the lower depths is only about 39 degrees Fahrenheit (4 degrees C).

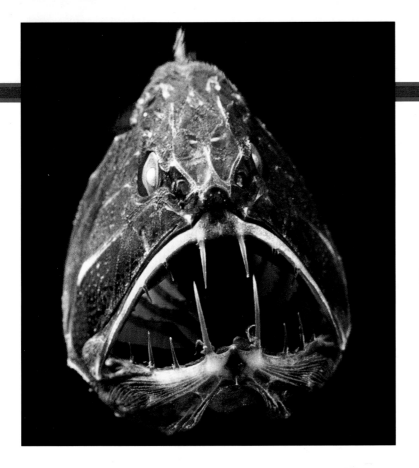

Fangtooths cruise through the water searching for their prey. And that may take awhile, because fewer animals swim in deep water than near the surface. Fangtooths eat small fishes, squids, and **crustaceans** (animals with jointed legs and hard shells). Shrimps, crabs, and lobsters are examples of crustaceans. A fangtooth's sharp fangs dig into its prey. Then the fangtooth gulps it down whole.

Most photographs of fangtooths do not include a ruler that measures the fish. When you see the huge teeth, you automatically assume that the fish must be very large, too. Not true. A fully grown fangtooth is only about 6 to 7 inches (15.2 to 17.8 cm) long.

An adult fangtooth is brown or brownish black. Younger fangtooths are a lighter shade of gray. Fangtooth **larvae** (newly hatched babies) live closer to the surface than adults do. As they grow up, they move into deeper water.

Fangtooths have fairly large eyes. Their eyes are especially good at seeing in darkness. People have special light sensitive cells, called **rods,** inside their eyes. Rods help us see in dim light. Fangtooths have lots of rods. Scientists think fangtooths may be able to see 15 to 30 times better than we can in dim light.

TARANTULAS

There are more than 700 species of tarantulas. They are found on every continent but Antarctica, and may be found in lowland regions as well as mountainous areas. The Mexican red-knee tarantula (Brachypelma smithii) lives in Mexico. These spiders became very popular as pets. So many have been captured and then sold in pet stores that they are becoming rare.

HAIRY HUNTERS

Some of the scariest scenes in movies involve tarantulas. They are the large, hairy **arachnids** (spiders) chosen to crawl upon the sleeping hero's pillow. The sight sends chills up many people's backs. If they only knew the truth! Tarantulas are not fierce at all. They are shy and seldom bite people. However, their fangs are sharp enough to give a painful bite.

It's this spider's size that probably scares people the most. We normally expect to see fingernail-size spiders outside our homes. A Mexican red-knee tarantula has a 1-inch-long (2.5 cm) body and a leg span of 3 to 4 inches (7.6 to 10 cm). Like the black widow, the Mexican red-knee tarantula **molts** (sheds its skin) several times before reaching its adult size.

This spider's eight brightly colored knees are only a short distance from the spider's body. Its legs grow from the front part of its body. Each of the legs ends in two hairy claws, which are used for walking and digging. The eyes, head, mouth, and fangs are also on this part of the spider's body. The abdomen forms the back part of its body. Its heart, lungs, and spinnerets are in this part. Hairs cover the spider's entire body. They are sensitive to air movements and help the spider determine what surrounds it. They also protect the body from rain.

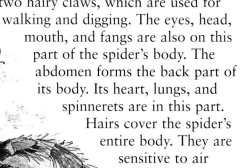

A Mexican red-knee tarantula does not live in a web. It digs a burrow into the ground. At the burrow's end, the spider carves out a room just big enough for its body. The spider waits just inside the **mouth** (opening) of its burrow until it senses prey. Then it hurries out and catches it.

The tarantula eats insects such as crickets and beetles. It may also eat small rodents, lizards, frogs, and small snakes. A tarantula's jaws are called **chelicerae** (kuh-LISS-uh-ruh). Each of these two hair-covered jaws has a fang attached. The fangs do not move like pincers, the way a black widow's do. Instead, a tarantula's fangs point downward. The spider rears up and slightly back to stab downward into its victim. Two short **pedipalps** (leg-like limbs) help the tarantula hold struggling victims. The fangs crush the victim's body against shorter teeth in the chelicerae.

Venom seeps into each fang from glands in the chelicerae and slows down the victim. Liquids strong enough to dissolve the prey's organs into slush are injected into its body. Next, special muscles around the tarantula's abdomen turn its stomach into a sucking machine. Hairs around the spider's mouth strain out any hard pieces from the prey's body.

Mexican red-knee tarantulas have a special defensive weapon, too. Some of the hairs on its abdomen have tiny **barbs** (hooks). When a predator threatens the spider, it rubs these hairs with its rear legs. The hairs shoot up and stick into the animal bothering the spider. The hairs are not poisonous, but the barbs dig into the skin, making it itch and sting for a few hours.

Mexican red-knee tarantulas are no threat to people. A bite is painful for a few days, but will not cause permanent harm. People, on the other hand, are a threat to the tarantula.

FANTASTIC FACT!

The Mexican red-knee tarantula is small when compared to its South American relative, the Goliath bird-eating tarantula. That spider's body is 3 inches (7.6 cm) across and its leg span may be close to 11 inches (28 cm)!

GIANT JAWS

Great white sharks (Carcharodon carcharias) can be found in ocean waters off the coast of most continents, except for Antarctica. They like temperate water, or water that's not too hot and not too cold. Most sharks prefer to live and hunt alone, not in groups, or even pairs.

Many species of fishes live in the earth's oceans. Few of them frighten people more than sharks. That's certainly understandable: sharks have sharp teeth. It's even more understandable when the teeth are inside the mouth of a great white shark. Great whites can grow to be about 20 feet (6 m) long. Maybe even larger.

A great white shark's skeleton is not made of bone like ours. Its skeleton is made of a softer material called **cartilage**. Your ears and the tip of your nose are made of cartilage. Most fishes have a swim bladder, a special organ that helps keep them afloat. Sharks do not have swim bladders. Cartilage weighs less than normal bone. That helps sharks stay afloat.

Great white sharks have very rough skin, like sandpaper. That's because their scales are different from other fishes' scales. A great white shark's scales are like tiny teeth. They stick up from the shark's skin and help protect its body from injury. These tiny tooth-like scales are called **denticles**. They are even covered with the same white, hard outer covering found on a tooth.

When a denticle is old and worn, it falls out. Denticles are continually shed and replaced.

A great white shark's teeth are actually modified, or changed, denticles. Over millions of years, the denticles around shark mouths grew larger and became specialized for ripping and tearing meat, a shark's main food. Each great white shark tooth has jagged edges that make it even more effective at cutting meat. A single tooth may be as long as 3 inches (7.6 cm).

Great whites have a fantastic sense of smell. One of the ways a shark finds prey is by following its nose. Great whites have no trouble smelling a few drops of blood or sea lion urine.

Once it senses prey, a great white shark begins the chase. When the time is right, the shark suddenly speeds up and grabs hold of the prey with its teeth.

Scientists who have studied great whites have noticed that after the shark takes its first bite, it usually **retreats** (backs off). The shark waits while the prey bleeds and becomes severely weakened or dies.

Then the shark bites again. This time it closes its mouth and shakes its head (and the prey's body) back and forth. The shark's teeth saw and cut through the victim's skin and bones.

Great white sharks do most of their hunting near the water's surface, rather than along the bottom. They prey on dolphins, sea lions, seals, rays, other fishes, and an occasional bird. They also eat dead whales and other dead animals they find floating in the water.

Unlike people, a great white shark has many rows of teeth. Teeth in the first row are near the shark's lips. Over time, they become dull, loosen, and fall out. That isn't a problem for the shark. There's a new tooth waiting to fill the space. The shark is ready for its next bite.

Great white sharks have attacked and killed people. And people have attacked and killed great white sharks. But each year people kill many more great whites than the other way around.

FANTASTIC FACT!

Sharks have special organs called the ampullae of Lorenzini. These organs sense electric fields. Every animal's body has an electric field. When a shark's ampullae sense a prey's field, the shark can zero-in for the kill.

SHORT-TAILED SHREWS

PARALYZING PREDATORS

Short-tailed shrews (Blarina brevicauda) can be found in most of the eastern and midwestern United States. They live in woods, fields, marshes, and bogs. Short-tailed shrews often live in backyard flower and vegetable gardens, where they may eat worms, slugs, and tiny frogs.

If you could shrink until you were only 1 inch (2.5 cm) tall, you would be the right size to explore a short-tailed shrew's runways, or tunnels. They wind under logs and through grasses, leaves, dirt, and snow. The only problem is, you might meet a short-tailed shrew. This small mammal is a fierce fighter. It has two fangs in the front of its mouth. Both fangs deliver a venomous bite.

Short-tailed shrews look a little bit like mice. Their short, dark-gray fur is soft. They have a long pointy nose, tiny eyes, and small ears. However, shrews are not rodents. Shrews belong to a large group of animals called **insectivores**, because many of their meals are insects.

Shrews live in burrows. They sometimes move into old burrows made by other animals. They are good diggers and can build their own burrow. A shrew's feet have five sharp claws. It uses them to scrape dirt from its runways and burrow. The shrew also uses its **snout** (nose) to push away dirt.

The short-tailed shrew's body produces a lot of energy. Its heartbeat races at a speed of 700 beats per minute. (Your heart beats 80 to 90 times per minute.) To keep a body like this healthy, a shrew must eat constantly. Scientists estimate that shrews eat 2 to 3 times their body's weight every day. They can be active during the day and at night.

A short-tailed shrew's tiny eyes really only distinguish light from dark. So when a shrew hunts, it relies on its keen sense of smell. It also uses its **vibrissae** (whiskers) to sense prey. A shrew's whiskers are very sensitive. They detect the air movements made by nearby prey. Vibrissae are sensitive to being touched. This helps a shrew avoid bumping into objects while scurrying about at night.

When a shrew attacks prey, it bites with its two large fangs, which can deliver venom.

A shrew's fangs are different from many fangs. A groove runs down the back of the fang instead of the front. Shrews can't inject venom forcefully, like a rattler, for example. The venom trickles down and into the cut made by the fang.

The venom is not strong enough to kill a person, but it may kill some prey. Much of the time the venom only stuns the prey so it can't escape. A shrew often carries its stunned prey home. The prey is stored for future meals.

Many animals hunt short-tailed shrews. Snakes, owls, and blue jays are a few of the animals that will catch and eat shrews. Shrews that live in backyard gardens are often killed by house cats. When a shrew is cornered, it fights furiously. While snapping at its enemy, it makes a lot of noise. Shrews make chirping noises, they twitter, and even buzz when they feel threatened. Their noises are loud enough to be heard many feet (meters) away.

FANTASTIC FACT!

The forefeet, head, and nose are all used to make tunnels. Shrews can burrow at the rate of nearly 12 inches (30 cm) per minute in soft soil.

VIPERFISHES

TRICKY TRAPPERS

Like fangtooths, viperfishes are deep-water fish. Most of us will only get to see viperfishes in photographs. And at first glance, a viperfish is nothing but fangs and more fangs.

The huge fangs in a viperfish's bottom jaw cause its mouth to hang open. When a viperfish does close its mouth, the fangs in its bottom jaw extend over its upper jaw. Along the edge, a viperfish's fangs are transparent, which may make them harder for prey to spot against the dark water surrounding the viperfish.

During the day viperfishes live in water that ranges from 1,600 to about 8,000 feet (488 to 2,438 m) deep. At night, viperfishes may swim to depths less than 1,000 feet (305 m) as they hunt for prey. Viperfishes eat small fishes and **invertebrates** (animals without backbones).

A viperfish has a clever way to attract prey to swim within range of its huge fangs. One of the rays on the fin on the viperfish's back is much longer than the others. The viperfish dangles this long, string-like ray over the front of its body.

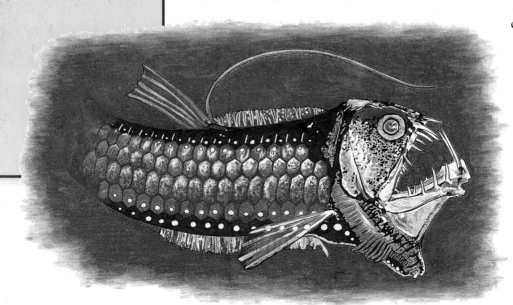

FANTASTIC FACT!

The water where viperfishes live is so deep that sunlight can't reach it. But a viperfish can make its own light. It has more than 350 light organs inside its mouth.

It wiggles the end, like a worm, in front of its mouth. When prey try to eat the viperfish's lure, it gets swallowed by the viperfish.

To catch prey, a viperfish moves its head and pushes its lower jaw forward. At the same time, its skull and the front part of its mouth move upward. (This is like turning your head to look up at the ceiling while opening your mouth.) As the viperfish swims forward, its prey is rammed into the viperfish's wide-open mouth. Fortunately, a viperfish's fangs bend slightly under pressure. Otherwise, the force of stabbing and ramming them into prey might break them.

When a viperfish swallows very large prey, its heart and other organs inside its body are moved aside. Special teeth in the viperfish's throat keep the prey moving along to the viperfish's stomach. The stomach stretches so the large prey will fit.

Viperfishes are **bioluminescent** (able to make light within their body). They have special light-producing organs called **photophores**. A viperfish has thousands of photophores on its body. Photophores on the underside of the viperfish may help to hide it from predators. When a predator, like a deep-water squid, looks upward, it is looking toward lighter water. It may not recognize the viperfish. Perhaps it will think the lighted area it sees is just lighter water.

The photophores inside a viperfish's mouth may confuse prey. The prey may think the light comes from an animal it would like to eat. When it swims near to investigate, the prey becomes the viperfish's meal instead.

Submersibles and other equipment used to explore the ocean depths are outfitted with lights. Scientists are concerned that the light from their machines may accidentally harm the animal's eyes. They are developing special lights that produce light rays that will not bother deep sea dwellers' eyes.

GRIZZLY BEARS

GREAT GROWLERS

Most grizzly bears (Ursus arctos horribilis) live in Alaska and western Canada. In smaller numbers they are also found in Wyoming, Montana, Washington, and Idaho. Grizzlies live in grassy river valleys, mountain meadows, and near coastal areas that have nearby wooded areas.

Many children like to cuddle with a teddy bear. Even though a grizzly bear may look cuddly, it isn't. First of all, it is big! A grizzly bear standing on all four feet is about 4 feet (1.2 m) high. But a large male standing up on his hind legs may be close to 10 feet (3 m) tall. That's higher than the ceiling in most houses. Also, a grizzly bear has four sharp canine teeth, sometimes called fangs, that are almost 3 inches (7.6 cm) long!

A grizzly's thick fur coat comes in a wide range of browns. Some are light enough to be called blond. Others are so dark they are almost black. A grizzly's fur looks frosted because the tips are colored gray or white. "Grizzled" means gray-haired, like the beard of an elderly man. That's how these bears got their name.

The hump on a grizzly bear's shoulder helps to distinguish it from black bears. A grizzly also has five claws on each paw. Each claw may be up to 4 inches (10 cm) long. One powerful swipe from a grizzly's front paw is enough to knock over a full-grown elk or bison.

In some northwestern rivers that feed into the ocean, salmon make seasonal swims upriver to lay their eggs. Grizzlies that live in those areas are superb fishers. A grizzly's sharp fangs are especially handy for grabbing and holding wiggly fish. A large grizzly can catch and eat more than 80 pounds (36 kg) of salmon in a day.

You may be surprised to learn that grizzlies also eat insects, such as army cutworm moths.

It may seem odd that grizzlies eat moths until you learn that an army cutworm moth's body is almost three-fourths fat. It also has a lot of protein, which is a good source of energy. Fat and protein help build the layer of fat a grizzly needs to survive hibernation.

A grizzly certainly has the power, claws, and teeth necessary to catch and kill large prey. But most of the time, it doesn't. A grizzly spends most of its feeding time eating plants. Like humans, grizzlies are **omnivores** (animals that eat both plants and meat).

A full-grown grizzly eats 25 to 35 pounds (11.25 to 15.75 kg) of food per day. Even though a grizzly bear has long, sharp fangs, plants and berries make up about 80 percent of its diet. The remaining 20 percent is meat.

Grizzlies do catch and kill prey—they often eat squirrels. Grizzlies also eat **carrion** (dead animals) that they find. Sometimes they steal dead prey from other animals.

FANTASTIC FACT!

Grizzlies do not eat or drink when they hibernate. A grizzly bear has to eat enough food during the summer and fall to nourish itself all winter. Some grizzlies build up a layer of fat 10 inches (25.4 cm) thick.

PROTECTING
FEROCIOUS FANGS

Many animal **populations** (groups) have had their numbers greatly reduced in the last 100 to 200 years. In the past, some people hunted too heavily. They killed thousands of animals. Sport hunting of grizzlies was very popular in the 1800s and early 1900s. Each year hundreds of eastern diamondback rattlesnakes are caught and killed during rattlesnake roundups. Great white sharks are trophy fish for sport anglers.

Habitat destruction is killing many animals. Habitat destruction occurs when the area where an animal normally lives and breeds is destroyed. Often, the animals it preys on are killed, or leave, because their homes are destroyed too. Most habitat destruction is caused by people.

When we build houses, stores, and roads we destroy many animal homes. When we build right on top of their homes, they have to move out. But they often don't go far. The animal's new home is likely to be close enough that the new people will stumble across them. And when people see them—like snakes—they often kill them.

Building roads ruins habitat in two ways. First, road construction tears apart animal homes. Second, roads give people easy access to the area. More human contact means more trouble for the animal.

Chemical pollution can also kill animals and destroy habitat. We are still studying what kind of impact our chemicals might be having on land animals and marine life.

Many of the species in this book are dangerous to people. And you might wonder why we should care about them. There are many reasons. For example, antivenin is used to cure snakebite. When injected into a person who has been bitten, the antivenin fights the venom's effects.

Some venom is used as a painkiller. Scientists are experimenting with venom as a treatment for certain nervous and circulatory system diseases. Sharks appear to be immune to cancer. Perhaps a cure can be found by studying great white sharks.

Insects, like flies and mosquitoes, carry and spread diseases. So do rodents. Rodents are also pests in a farmer's fields and food storage sheds. They eat and defecate on the stored crop. Many of these ferocious fang animals are great natural insect and rodent killers.

Perhaps the best reason for saving these animals is that we don't know what will happen to the environment once they are gone. Together, animal and plant life affect the appearance and the health of the place they live. And if they all die, there's no way to bring them back.

All animals deserve our respect. As long as people are careful and behave properly when we are in their territory, both humans and animals—including those with ferocious fangs—can survive.

Great Sunburst Baboon Tarantula

Some animals have fangs to either protect themselves or to help in the capture of their next meal. While these animals may not look or act like most of the animals with which you are more familiar, it doesn't mean we should appreciate them any less. They are using these special "tools" in order to survive and eventually produce another generation. Here are some more "ferocious fangs" from around the world. You may want to learn more about them, too!

MORE
FEROCIOUS FANGS

SPITTING COBRA
(*Naja mossambica*)
The hole in this African snake's fang is not at the tip. It is midway down the front of the fang. A spitting cobra's fangs spray venom outward at the snake's victim.

LION
(*Panthera leo*)
Lions have four sharp fangs. They are used to kill prey and bite off chunks of flesh. All the teeth in a lion's mouth are sharply pointed. Lions are found in parts of Africa and one place in Asia.

BROWN RECLUSE
(*Loxoceles reclusa*)
A brown recluse spider's venomous fangs pinch together, like a black widow's. Brown recluses live in the United States.

SPOTTED HYENA
(*Crocuta crocuta*)
The hyena is best known for its peculiar "bark" that sounds like hysterical laughter. But a hyena's fangs are no laughing matter. They easily crush through large bones. The spotted hyena lives in Africa.

TASMANIAN DEVIL
(*Sacrophilus harrisii*)
Tasmanian devils live on the island of Tasmania, which is part of Australia. They are fierce fighters and have sharp fangs. The female carries her babies in a pouch on her belly.

GABOON VIPER
(*Bitis gabonica*)
This venomous snake, found in Africa, has fangs that are 2 inches (5 cm) long. Fortunately, they are calm snakes. They must be really angry (or hungry) before they bite.

HIPPOPOTAMUS
(*Hippopotamus amphibius*)
People in Africa have great respect for hippos and their gigantic canine teeth. The teeth are only used for fighting and slashing predators. Hippos are easily angered and will attack animals and people who annoy them.

WOLVERINE
(*Gulo gulo*)
Wolverines look like small bears with long tails. Their sharp fangs have no trouble ripping a victim's body into pieces. They live in the northern parts of Europe, North America, and Asia.

KOMODO DRAGON
(*Varanus komodoensis*)
Growing more than 10 feet (3 m) long, the komodo dragon is the world's largest lizard. It has razor-sharp teeth and preys on small deer and wild pigs. It lives in Indonesia.

KILLER WHALE
(*Orcinis orca*)
This streamlined ocean swimmer is really a member of the dolphin family. Its large mouth is filled with sharp white teeth. Killer whales live in oceans all around the world.